Hell Is A Cage In Heaven

Allen James

ALLEN JAMES

ISBN-9781093374995

Dedicated to my family
who I am fortunate to call *friends*,
And the friends
who I am fortunate to call *family*.

CONTENTS

ALLEN JAMES

You came to me,
Like words to a song,
Touched every memory,
But the feeling was gone,
Watched me carry myself,
With courage and grace,
Noticed nothing was heavier,
Than a smiling face,
Witnessed days turn to years,
By the wand in the clock,
Yet the magic of time,
Couldn't make the pain stop,
Surely you understood,
As far as eyes could see,
But a crumbling soul,
Leaves no debris,

No divine purpose,
No lessons to learn,
Some Gods,
Just want to watch a man burn,
So now I follow the words,
Of a wise, holy liar,
For when the truth sets you free,
It sets you on fire.

ALLEN JAMES

As Real As Pain

I want the kind of love,
That's just as real as pain,
The kind you don't recover from,
Nor want to anyway,
An elated sense of presence,
Like needles through a hand,
Breathing at the mercy,
Of my heart's every command,

The sweet rush of adrenaline,
From stepping on a nail,
How it grabs my blood's attention,
And keeps my armor frail,
And if I should be so lucky,
To have the state of sharp pain linger,
I hope one day you'll meet me,
The way a hammer meets a finger.

Temple

For nights she waited
at the doorstep of arousal,
Held tightly in a fabric
of a fantasy she wore.
Only to walk inside
and join the morning prayer,
At the holy segregation
of a woman and her clothes.

A thousand old truths,
Which one will you choose?
Don't ever confuse,
The truth for a promise,
They'll promise you lies,
And lies never die,
Only the liars…

If you know yourself.
For knowledge is power,
Of seconds and hours,
And climb up the tower,
Of tumbling giants,
Go jump off the shoulders,
And wake up to silence,
So lay down your eyelids,
Every kingdom is sold,
For the rite price,
Unseen from the world,
Kings and their queens,

We spend our lives
trying to fill that
which is infinite,

And then wonder
why we're so exhausted.

- The Void

Hell Is A Cage In Heaven

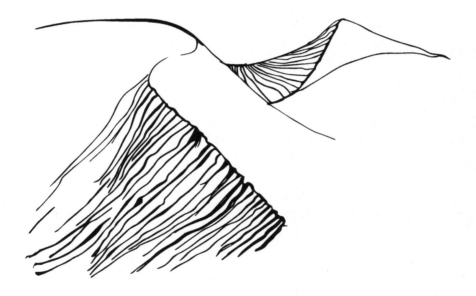

Take a walk alone,
On these desert rocks,
Let yourself be stranded,
From everything you're not,
For where there's one,
There can be two,
So let yourself be empty,
Like the desert we walk through,

Give up all you know,
Of who you think you are,
Release your captured echoes,
At the edges of your heart,
And do not pity those,
Who have nothing left to drink,
Better to be empty,
When the watchful sky will wink.

- *Empty*

Like the moment I first saw her,
Parched lips that tasted water,
Mother nature's only daughter,
Living on the street,

In the open desert valley,
I feel her air around me,
Effortless and soundly,

One day we will meet.

You're my joy,
And my grief,
My peaceful rest,
And lack of sleep,
My only truth,
My endless fraud,
You're my heathen,
And my God,
My brightest future,
And dark past,
You're my first love,
And my last,
The source of sickness,
And good health,
A stranger and,
My deepest self,
My rising sun,
And fallen moon,
You're the dreadful silence,
And my favorite tune,
You are my numbness,
And my pain,
My peace of mind,
And thoughts unchained,
My heart of gold,
Split in two,
Good or bad,
I dream of you.

The Dogs Know How To Die

I used to wake up every morning,
With life's mascot at my feet,
He'd lick the frown right off my face,
And joyous words his eyes would speak,

For they were like two windows,
From which I could not hide,
And every time he looked at me,
Light made its way inside,

Each day was new and full of wonder,
Every thread of grass was his,
He had the world inside a ball,
And to chase it was pure bliss,

Oh sweet and playful days,
Memories I recall,
I wonder if he misses them,
Or remembers them at all,

For the morning's generosity,
Has finally run dry,
Warm and sunny afternoons,
Are now the cruelest time,

The food his nose once blindly followed,
Now rots before his sight,
How there is no pain in hunger,
Without an appetite for life,

Each night I lay beside him,
And try to keep his eyes alert,
But I see them fading slowly,
Like the paw prints in the dirt,

Surely he must know it,
In every aching bone,
It's why he crawls into the corner,
And lies there all alone,

Gone are the endless days,
Of chasing rabbits in the hedge,
No matter what the game is,
Life's a stick he will not fetch,

Oh brother to my soul,
Not even a goodbye?
When there's no more life to live,
The dogs know how to die.

Silly little wishes,
Fantasies and dreams,
Who but me to make them true?
Or so that way it seems,
Twice a day, a minute spent,
Begging my soul's master,
Oh I could count a thousand prayers,
Without a single answer,
Kneeling down on tender knees,
Beneath a tightly knotted rope,
Wishful truth may set me free,
But the cruelest lie is hope,
So of these vacant, mystic promises,
I've grown weary and suspicious,
If I am God, then God is dead,
And so are all my wishes.

Before I declare myself an optimist
or pessimist,

I'd like to know what's in the cup.

The thought of loving you

runs through my mind,
Creating memories
of a past that never happened,
Imagining a future
that will never come to be,
Living in the present moment
of a dream.

It's haunting me tonight,
A ghost begging to be seen,
But every time I touch it,
Empty hands are all I feel,

Reality is calling,
Love makes schizophrenics of us all.

God is a woman,
The world cannot hide,
All of her children,
Will lover her in time,

Ten commandments,
Written on her thigh,
God is a woman,
And heaven is her lie,

I worship her blindly,
Just to see her again,
No prayers inside me,
But I say "Amen",

On my knees,
I've been begging every night,
Waiting for the love,
Of my after life,

And I'll carry my sins,
To the gates of hereafter,
An eye for an eye,
And tears for her laughter,
Follow every last word,
For as long as I'm human,
If love is a religion,
Then God is a Woman.

- God Is A Woman

Death is waiting for me
　　　downstairs in the car.

　　　But I'm running late as always,

　　　　　　　Old habits,
　　　　　　　　They die hard.

Hell Is A Cage In Heaven

The Artist

Her gospel beauty rises early,
Yet always late to gratify,
With eyes that gleam with intuition,
They burn the shelter where thoughts hide,
Her creativity runs circles,
Around these worthless, old commandments,
And so new love approaches me,
The way a painter does a canvas.

Day 1

The moment you came into this world,
I was born in yours,
Nurtured by your beauty,
Held safely in your palm,
I smiled as I gazed
into those bright, fascinated eyes,
Realizing how long it's been
since I last saw through them.

With every shallow breath,
You filled my lungs with air,
Every drop of tear,
Bathing my heart anew,
Brought into a home,
Where even guardian angels sleep,

On this very day,
My life began.

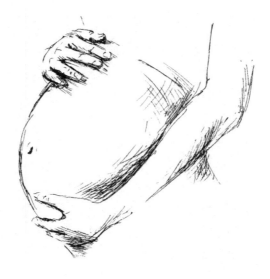

Witness from eternity,
As many lies as one can tell,
For any man who'd die for you,
Must live for you as well,
Enjoy the company of roses,
And sweet perfume of second love,
With each new dream your heart imposes,
An ancient truth you can speak of,
Let fairy tales be written,
Even if they'll one day burn,
For moments only turn to ashes,
If the pages aren't turned,
Do not be damned by those who've wronged you,
Or whose ever heart you have eschewed,
There's only one God you belong to,
And his name is Gratitude,
Be patient with your sense of longing,
Indulge your wisdom as it comes,
And listen closely when it's calling,
For they'll be days you can't outrun,
Live every second of the hour,
Even when it's filled with pain,
For in surrender lies the power,
To know your soul cannot be tamed,
And should you choose these words to live by,
Or turn your back and walk away,
There's just one thing you must remember,
It's that I love you anyway.

I'm in no rush
to write my masterpiece,
Taking my time
with gentle hands,
And all of these words
that never seem to meet,
Fly away
to be caught again.

- Firefly

Poems In The Sky

I know that I have left you,
Like the tears that leave your eyes,
And that my beating heart,
Was once your lullaby,

I know that I've surrendered,
Yet you're the one who lost,
Left to pay the price,
With the coin that I have tossed,

I know your world feels empty,
And your heart fills with despair,
Each time you turn to look my way,
And see nobody there,

But I'm hoping that you'll notice,
Once this tender time has passed,
These words that I have left you with,
Were surely not the last,

For if you listen softly,
You'll never hear me say *goodbye*,
With all my love I write to you,
Poems in the sky.

Like the stars
that shine at night,
Our bodies die,
But not our light.

Brother

Walk beside me, brother,
Show me where the river ends,
Where the hidden paths assemble,
And where I should begin,
Tell me why the lone wolf howls,
And why the birds fly side by side,
Draw the stars in shapes of owls,
And watch me closely from the sky,
Help me climb the ancient trees,
Where the nameless fruits still grow,
Make two spears for us to hunt with,
Like we once did years ago,
Summon stories of our ancestors,
And of the places you have been,
Share the secrets of the forest,
That are spoken by the wind,
Point me to the shapeless casket,
Where the mourning soul is healed,
Whisper gently of death's magic,
And tell me how it feels,
Leave your footsteps at the causeway,
With every lesson you have shown,
And promise me, my brother,
I'll one day get there on my own

So Long

You lived for the truth,
And you died for it too,
An old, poet's heart,
You could not renew,

You spoke every last secret,
Every broken hallelujah,
In a tower for two,
Is where I once knew you,

You sang in a whisper,
Heavy as gold,
In a suit that was tailored,
For the largest of souls,

And though we never shared thoughts,
Over oranges and tea,
This entire time,
You've spoken to me,

Through mountains of words,
Carried by song,
Now it's my turn,
To tell you "So long",

The Holy Ghost,
The miracle passed,
Each grain of time,
Your voice will outlast,

You wanted it darker,
But your light won't depart,
It has found its way,
Through the cracks in my heart,

And so if it is true,
Everything that you say,
Then maybe there's a God above,
And I'll meet you someday.

In memory of Leonard Cohen

The door to freedom opened,
Yet there he still remained,
For the will to fly has atrophied,
And the bird is finally caged.

Mirror, Mirror

Tell me about your wicked past,
Your history,
Your life gone fast,
I'm waiting for you, baby,
Like an organ,

I'm here with God in his hotel,
And *man*
he really looks like hell,
Brother it ain't easy
being worshiped.

Mirror, mirror on the wall,
You're laughing at us,
Aren't ya doll,
I know it's always ugly
from your corner,

Let's get high,
And let's fall down,
It doesn't matter anyhow,
The world keeps spinning,
It's making me feel nauseous,

I finally see the point of life,
It's sharper than a kitchen knife,
Stick me with it, baby,
Like I taught you,

Let's dig up another grave,
They say the dead don't misbehave,
But I keep looking
over my cold shoulder,

No one's left inside this place,
But I'm still smiling, just in case,
I need you, baby,
Like a soul needs torture.

Another chance
to meet again,
Let's start over
at the end,
And dust the ashes
of a rose,
Our love will never
decompose.

- *The Garden*

I've swallowed every tear,
That sat upon your lips,
Following their trails,
On gentle manuscripts,
They've led me to a place,
Only few have seen,
An ocean full of pain,
That prides a deep blue green,
I've felt the beat of sadness,
As I laid upon your chest,
And listened to a tune,
That would never let you rest,
Two separated hands,
Whose fingers interlaced,
Going down a road,
Our paths have never faced...

What are we in search of,
If not death's counterpart?
Let the arrows guide us,
And not shoot our reckless hearts,
And if we end up damaged,
Like we never have before,
Then at least we'll know for certain,
That we won't hurt any more.

I hate to disappoint you, darling,
But I'm no brave knight,
Only a curious fool.

Anyway Café

On a blue agave current,
Drifts the August night,
With a scent of summer's sweet perfume,
And allure of firelight,
Seated at the holy table,
Where the old souls used to pray,
Now their spirits come to life,
At the Anyway Café,

Angels dancing with their shadows,
Waiting to be loved,
But if you ever get too close,
They'll be pulled by the reigns above,
Vessels for a melody,
In the future we rejoice,
Echoing the history,
Of the man with a golden voice.

POW

The rapid fire of a printer,
Can rip a soul to shreds,
At 9:00AM some think it's ten,
While others just forget,

One by one, we hold our ground,
With nowhere to retreat,
Our fingers march in unison,
To the sound of the same beat,

Young Billy is in the corner,
Still trembling in his boots,
This is no place for tender hearts,
For that is what we shoot,

12:00PM - lay down your pen,
All soldiers must be fed,
A busy stomach takes the mind,
Off battlefields ahead,

Fly back now birdie, it's twelve thirty,
There's been a breach of internet,
The ranks all break, as someone yells,
"Run for your cigarettes!"

Pull yourselves together now!
There's glory to be had,
They say our names will live forever,
When sales aren't too bad,

4:00PM - it's time again,
To reassess our plan,
All team leaders to the front,
In chains of old command,

Let's push a little further now,
One well-oiled machine,
We'll break our backs, our necks, our wrists,
But we will never break routine!

6:00PM - we did it men,
Victory is here!
Now how about we celebrate?
And drink away the years,

But wait a second, look out there,
The enemy's not through!
I know they're all too young to die,
But killing children is what we do,

Another round - what say you now?
Let's not forget our cause,
So many bodies have been found,
But all the minds are lost,

So brace yourselves for madness,
Thoughts of discharge from your desk,
For delusion earns no payment here,
And hopes are kept in check,

And if you ever dare to wander,
Then you too may go berserk,
With visions of a POW,
A prisoner of work.

Absence

Like a warm, winter blanket,
Stripped from a naked shoulder,
Her heart yearns evermore,
While mine only grows colder.

Missing Child

I opened up a window,
And the wind came rushing in,
Knocking over promises,
And photographs of him,
I closed my eyes for just a moment,
And in that moment he was gone,
They say *don't bother trying to find him,*
It's just been far too long,
But the dust won't settle lightly,
And this house will not burn down,
So I'll keep looking out the window,
Until the roof is underground.

There goes the rain,
Her gentle lover,
The only one,
Who's ever touched her,
From head to toe,
And deep inside,
In shapeless arms,
She comes alive.

A name was stitched together,
With corporate cloth in every letter,
And although I had once met her,
I read it carefully,
She asked to take my order,
From her side of the border,
Like shelter from a mortar,
Of a familiar enemy,

Our time was passed in silence,
Amid fear's warm defiance,
While chances shut like eyelids,
A dream I slept away,
Now the nights do not come kindly,
They only bring the days behind me,
With thoughts that travel blindly,
And words I'll never say.

- Christina

I walked into an empty room today,
How quietly it was all swept away,
Took a seat and played our tune,
Strummed on the dust of bitter ruins,
Where songs were born,
And memories lived,
Can't help but think,
What made you give?
The soul in you,
The hole in me,
The walls that keep us apart,
Years will pass,
And I'll remember,
The day you sold your beating heart.

- 2/17/2013

ALLEN JAMES

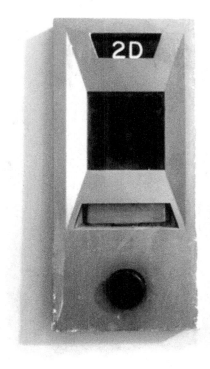

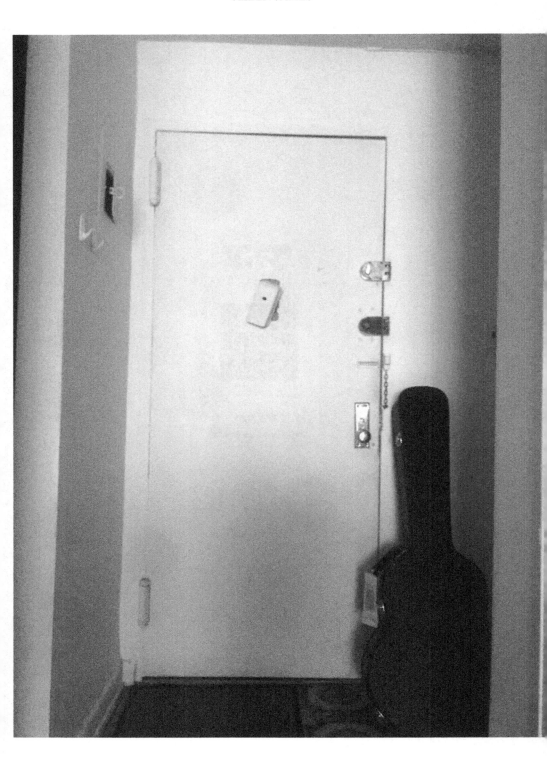

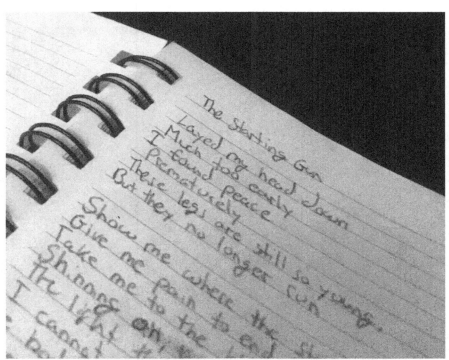

The Starting Gun

Layed my head down
Much too early
I found peace
Prematurely
These legs are still so young,
But they no longer run

Show me where the
Give me pain to end
Take me to the li
Shining ah
The light
I cannot t

Midnight Thoughts ...

Ask me how I'm doing
and I'll make it sell,
Tell you all is well,
When all is hell,
Falling through the sky,
Didn't hit the ground yet,
Just me and God here,
Playing Russian roulette,
The wage is set,
A bet's a bet,
Final stages of rage,
But my mind won't reset,

I'm a mental vegan,
Only seeking raw truth,
Had a residence in present tense,
And the future on mute,
Now I turn to the past,
With a promise to face it,
My word is gold,
Not some fake ass bracelet,

Three steps to forgiveness,
But life ain't a waltz,
It's a dance with the devil,
And he leads till you're lost,
You see I paid the cost,
And got nothing back,
But pages of thoughts and a midnight snack,

They call it "hell and back"
Well the hell with that,
I'll be burning for my sins,
No matter what the habitat,
Fully packed and ready to die,
I'm ditching this life,
Like a runaway bride,
Too young to hide,
So I hurried up and got old,
Now my back hurts,
From all the anger I hold,

I'm close to the edge,
Yet far from a heathen,
The only reason I left heaven,
Was to make peace with my demons.
Problem is,
They just want to get even,
And now I'm barely breathing,
Barely sleeping at night,
So to answer your question,
No, I'm not alright.

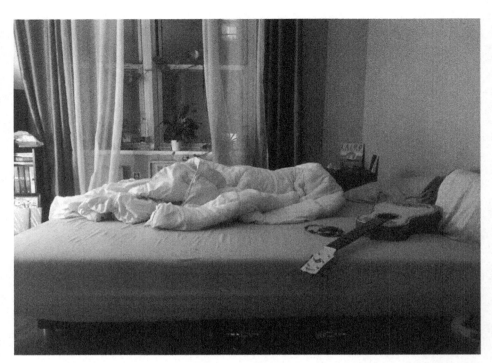

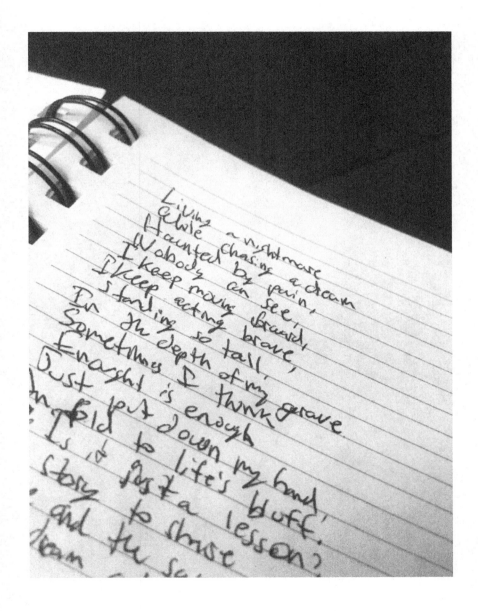

I reduce my pen to a sword
and violently penetrate the naked page.

At last,
An honest poem.

A Touch Of Madness

I've got a woman in my bed,
Another in my heart,
Got roses colored red,
And they're falling apart,
Well I know the sweetest sunshine,
Comes after the rain,
But don't you know by now?
I'm in love with the pain,

Hurt me with your silence,
I'll only wish you well,
You're just a little angel,
Who's been through hell,
So kiss me with your lies,
Touch me without proof,
But when you're in my bed,
I want you naked like the truth.

You're running around in circles,
Looking for romance,
Has no one ever told you?
Love's a dance,
You're trying to remember,
What I tried to forget,
You better quit me now,
Like you did your cigarettes,

Such a pretty penny,
For the health I had to pay,
But darling I'm still begging,
For a different kind of change,
You said the moon was ours,
But you've had it for days,
Oh the hell with the damn thing,
I never liked it anyway.

A touch of madness comes
with every step you take my way,
All this time
I feared the silence,
But it had so much to say.

I've held gentle hands,
And felt a moment in time,
Yet all I could think,
Was how she felt holding mine,
And though heart had been taken,
Her beauty was free,
I did not want to be with her,
I simply wanted to be.

Angels

To a heavenly whisper,
I followed their tracks,
But once a step had been taken,
There was no turning back,
All those promising faces,
Yet how could I tell?
My guiding light shined,
From a fire in hell,
Two-faced magicians,
Pulling love from a hat,
By the time I received it,
My heart spoiled black,
Seems this life I've been chasing,
Is tied to a string,
I keep juggling hope,
For the laughs of a king,
Where the muse becomes master,
In this clever old trap,
I've been blessed with a gift,
That I cannot unwrap,
So I gaze to the stars,
Every tale meant to be,
Envisioning dreams,
That do not see me,
Just another cruel circle,
Around sleepless remains,
I don't trust these damn angels,
Only torment and pain.

Healing is a peasant's dirty work,
Not fit for royalty,

And I must admit,
I'm the king of drama queens.

The devil, he may sin,
But he's a southern gentleman,
With open doors,
His home is yours,
No God's more welcoming
than him.

- Orphan

The Two Travelers

Rarer than radium,
And they tried to find,
A droplet of anyone,
Who'd give them a ride,
Past the sweet smell of home,
Through the treacherous mind,
They were soon all alone,
In the remnants of time,

No destination,
No hope of return,
Just an old inclination,
They could not adjourn,
A map without lines,
Directing the course,
Read *You must run for miles*
to walk through the doors,

So they ran and they ran,
Crawled and they climbed,
Till the shadows they cast,
Were left far behind,
And all they could see,
Was an old, widowed soul,
Down by the river,
Where its story was told,

But the words of a breeze,
Quickly grew into storms,
As death soon approached them,
In all shapes and form,
With nowhere to run,
They now greeted farewell,
Singing endless duets,
To the mademoiselle,

Patiently waiting,
For the night to be purged,
When at last, an hour was spewed,
And their path had diverged,
Illuminating before them,
A road split in two,
One that went back,
And one that went through,

So they followed their truth,
Instead of their eyes,
To the mirrors of youth,
Where no man can see lies,
Up in the stars,
With both feet on the ground,
And when they took their next step,
Each other they found.

Dedicated to don Howard Lawler

ALLEN JAMES

Freedom is a stranger,
And I am but a child,
Heeding the panic
of a mother's love.

The Death Of A Parent

She's pacing back and forth,
In the isle between hope and despair,
Trying to make sense of the unimaginable,
Her hands scratch away,
As if some sort of answer lies beneath her skin,
For the house is always clean,
Each meal prepared too quickly,
Even the television, her reliable companion,
Provides no comfort in this time of need.

She knows that she is dying,
The death of every parent,
Dreadfully afraid,
To become a child once more.

The Rising Sunset

It was some sort of trickery,
The world played upon my eyes,
When the setting sun before me,
Suddenly began to rise,
And the time that once flew swiftly,
Had somehow been reversed,
Like a spell out of a fairy tale,
That had broken life's old curse,
How preciously the world was saving,
The light that almost died,
As I marveled at the miracle,
Shining in the sky,
And so it marveled back at me,
As it enticed a thought to think,
That perhaps the sun is setting,
And I'm just catching up to it.

Whispering to calm me down
as you wash the stains of history,
How desperately I've tried
to turn my life around,

But all roads lead into your arms again.

More Than Life

You're the needle in my arm,
Give me pleasure,
Do me harm,
Show me heaven,
Past the light,
Where death loves me,
More than life,

Break my skin,
And take what's yours,
Leave me,
While I still want more,
Just like death,
For you I wait,
More than life,
We can create.

We were more than life,
Where tomorrow never kisses
yesterday goodbye,
More than life,
And we'll soak up every moment
until the day goes dry.

She pours her heart out
like a hot cup of tea,
Helplessly inconsiderate
of those beside her.

There's an old man inside me,
Waiting to die,
He sits by the window,
And sees the world going by,
Each night he retires,
With a film to unwind,
Watching the war flicks,
That play in my mind,
When will his time come?
I may never know,
But impatience is a child,
That time slowly grows,
Perhaps one of these days,
As he drifts softly to sleep,
I'll come take his life,
And keep it discrete,
For I've longed to inherit,
What is rightfully mine,
Wasting away,
In a home I can't find.

- *Rightful Owner*

Here lies the victor,
Whose crown has appeared,
Not placed on his head,
But grown through the years,
With diamonds and gold,
And fabulous rings,
A peasant's reward,
For the madness of kings.

Big Bad World

Little boy,
Have you been outside?
Is there anybody left
for you to find?
Are you still out there
on your feet?
Everybody hides,
But nobody ever seeks,

I see the children playing after dark,
In their ten by ten inch park,

I hear the cries of empty swings,
Back and forth
they're pushed on by the wind,
Another frame around a face
who's seen the world,
But never got a taste,

I feel the memories drifting far away,
It's up to you, kid,
Save the day.

Little boy, don't you fear the night,
It's a big bad world,
But it's on your side,
Little girl with the pale blue eyes,
One day the world will turn,
For you and I.

Tree Of Life

When days are long and nights are longer,
And dreams become the fear of sleep,
When doubt and hopelessness are growing stronger,
And the climb before you never looked so steep,
When a brittle branch provokes your ponder,
And makes you want to turn around,
When motion stops and mind begins to wander,
Remember why you left the ground,

When looking down sparks fear inside you,
And looking up is done so desperately,
When dizzy heights begin to blind you,
Into yourself you now must see,
When daunting voices yell below you,
Urging you to come on down,
When not one soul is left to guide you,
Embrace the freedom you have found,

When tired arms cannot continue,
At the very moment you've been striving for,
Grab ahold the hand of sinew,
And watch how far your strength will soar,
And when you wake upon one quiet morning,
With sun-kissed apples at your every bite,
You'll find it's not the fruit,
But the view that's most rewarding,
And you'll have climbed the tree of life.

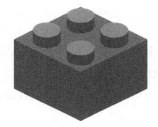

The Creative Child

When I was young
I spawned universes out of sand,
Made companions out of stones,
And won epic battles
with only a few good plastic men,

And so when my toys were traded
for life's unexpected challenges,
I did what I do best,
And created a catastrophe.

Passing By

Lady-killers dancing
with the overnight romantics,
The fragrant taste of antics rising high,
And a drink or two
to think things through,
For every trail here intersects,
With fat checks
and mirrors under lines,

But the liquor flows from upside down,
Through the men and up the women's gown,
And not a single vacant room in town,
Just the *One Night Visit* sign,
And a man up front who makes the deal
says, "You can touch but you can't feel",
And I must admit it does appeal,
But I'll let it pass me by.

Good ole' Brandy's looking fancy,
A poor old sack in sight,
The angel's kiss fills him with bliss,
And so he grabs her tight,
In walks Big John, and he ain't too fond
of men who turn their backs,
And Mrs. Daniels,
She likes Samuel,
But she'd rather dance with Jack,

Johnny Walker resting
on a pair of risky aces,
The whisky hints the raises
amply with the deuce,
And he took the bait
cause he couldn't see straight,
A sip, a slip, a loss of grip,
And suddenly all hell breaks loose,

Rampantly the cowboys
come storming on white horses,
The eternal moonshine in their mighty roar,
And nobody ever stopped
for the warning shot,
So they fire off until they got
this high and mighty place
dropped to the final floor.

And the riders came from inside out,
Through the Inn and went on about,
When they asked me why I took this route,
I told my little lie,
But the awful truth, it stays intact,
You can't erase this faded fact,
Take one good look and turn my back,
And keep on passing by.

ALLEN JAMES

I've burned the last Kingdom
with Jesus inside,
To the ashes of a phoenix,
Where nothing can rise,
Scorched the seminal wings
of every angel I need,
A garden destroyed
by the fear of a seed.

There lies an anxious candle,
Whose flame is never still,
It shudders and it staggers,
As it's held against its will,

But the more it tries to struggle,
The quicker it will burn,
Like a mouse inside a bucket,
Whose milk it cannot churn,

The wax on which it's standing,
Grows less with every night,
As the flame continues sinking,
On measurements of life,

Each grain of light is fleeting,
Erasing lines from my palm,
The pleasant scent it has been weaving,
No longer keeps it calm,

Teased by moving shadows,
That make it yearn so desperately,
For the mercy of sweet darkness,
To come and set it free,

Burning through each memory,
On charred and faded glass,
It's finally reached the bottom,
With no time left to pass,

A shriveled, little ember,
With a tiny spark of doubt,
I let it flicker one last time,
And blow the candle out.

- *The Candle*

The mere thought of the beast
unlocks his cage.

I forced myself to bear
what nature's laws won't tolerate,
And looked into the eyes
of the raging bull headed for us all,
I stared too long and reached too far,
Until I felt an everlasting peace
 swiftly sever from my soul,
For what was once a distant folktale,
Now crawls out from the pages,
Every pretty face,
A mirror for the ugly truth,
And so I cast my thoughts in all directions,
In hopes of catching glimpses
of a bottomless pursuit.

- Hyper Extension

Stranger

Talk to me in signs
like the angels do,
How they cry for you
to stay,
Memories of a child,
But the moment's gone,
No, you don't belong
to me.

The Art Of Love

You swing your words carelessly,
Both truth and lies,
Viciously smiling,
With that look in your eyes,
The glorious raid,
Of all who can bleed,
Your one claim to fame,
A red carpet, indeed,
How faithful they are,
To the apple of man,
For all who dare fight,
Are yours to command,
As you sit and admire,
Yourself from their view,
Another statue erected,
That looks nothing like you,
Our darling illusion,
The starving oasis,
You've hidden yourself,
Behind all the right places.

The Feet Of A Thousand Dreams

Alone
in my bones,
While she lies
with the night,

Stains
of her soul,
Only time
will survive,

Pray
for the sun
to slow down
when she's kind,

Dragged
through the clouds,
Just the price
for a ride.

And the way that she lies
at the edge of my life,
Where the hills meet the howling sea,
And as the world walks away,
My heart begs to stay
at the feet of a thousand dreams.

Beggar

Angel in my bed,
Devil in my head,
A beggar's dying,
And I'm wishing I were him,
But God won't let me in,
No he says keep trying,

I keep trying…

Brother to my soul,
You walk the street alone,
So tired of fighting,
And it hurts to see you here,
With nothing left to fear,
It's terrifying,

Old man in the wild,
What happened to you, child?
They still can't find you,
Now a witness to the breeze,
You're singing on your knees,
But the words keep lying.

And the years have gone,
No one saw,
But the sun that brings tomorrow,
Promise me,
Anything at all.

Surrender

Let go

Release

And be free

But how to let go

of that which holds me?

She knew better
than to leave her heart unattended,
As it had been spiked many times before,
But her curious mind dared to wander,
Leaving the familiar blur
to come softly dripping in,
And now a bitter alchemy awaits her,
Like a patient stalker, hiding in the night,
Floating in a silent celebration,
Of the great illusion's
sweet return.

I'm running free
in sweet exile,
Living like
nobody's child,
Once bound in shame,
But now I see,
A Godless world
is heavenly.

And though I know
that you will miss me,
In the winter's lonely season,

It will never mean you love me,
For love is its own reason.

Hell Is A Cage In Heaven

Eternal Sun

I am the eternal sun,
You are the earth and sky,
If I ever get too close,
I know you'll surely die,

So I must keep a cold restraint,
With burning flames of sinew,
And paint a shadow of your grace,
To vicariously walk with you,

And you will take from me my warmth,
In ways you cannot see,
As you make your way through life,
Without ever loving me,

And so I wait for night to blind me,
As I lie here and remember,
The fleeting seconds of horizon,
Where your beauty lasts forever,

Only to rise another day,
In which I'm cursed to shine,
Knowing you're the only light,
That will never become mine.

Uma,
Darling hoped to see you soon,
Your ghost is here tonight,
Just to hear me play a song or two,

Uma,
Why'd you take your silver spoon?
Down on the alley floor,
I tried to stab this life right into you.

Uma,
You're dying but it's nothing new,
Down on the alley floor,
You couldn't see me standing over you,

Uma,
You could've been a woman soon,
Lying here with me,
In between the sun
and the moon.

Uma,
Darling don't you cry for me,
I am the one
who has to shed your tears
Oh Uma,
Won't you try to see?
I am the one
who makes you appear.

ALLEN JAMES

Love ain't a spell,
It's a magic trick,
You're fooling around
just to practice it,
Yes, love is a game,
But the sad thing is,
You never play
for happiness.

A naked body is all she knows,
For no man dares undress her soul.

The Flight

In the heart of the jungle,
The truth always lies,
A dozen paths you could walk,
That will lead you inside,
But I chose to fly,
On a marvelous plane,
Soaring over the trees,
That were calling my name,
Landing quite roughly,
On all I hoped for and more,
A fertile land,
That grew wisdom galore,
But what I had realized,
After many fine nights,
Was that this remote place,
Had no return flights,
And so the time came,
When I had to go back,
And once again stood before me,
A dozen old paths,
Foreign only for those,
Who've not travelled by foot,
And now I'm out here alone,
Forever lost in the woods.

ALLEN JAMES

Hell Is A Cage In Heaven

What is darkness?
But a servant of the light,
For each star shines,
By virtue of the night.

No Son Of Mine

You had a good old time,
Left the whole damn world behind,
There's no grave,
Like the hole you made,
No, you ain't no son of mine,

God is getting old,
And no devil wants your soul,
So if you want to die,
Well don't be shy,
There ain't nobody home,

How you let the minutes pass,
As if your life was built to last,
Ain't no Lord,
You can afford,
Unless you pay him back in ash,

No, you ain't no son of mine,
You ain't no son of mine,

You can kiss the sky,
Until you're divine,
But you ain't no son of mine.

I've read the ancient scriptures,
And memorized each sonnet,
Like a whore I laid in bed,
With every mystic, sage, and prophet,
Slowly earned my winds of change,
To buy the promise of a ring,
But there is no lie as clever,
As the faithful bride of spring,
So I ask myself at every end,
Has wisdom made a fool of me?
To lead me to the great ascend,
And shatter both my knees,
To hang my wits above me,
In a tightly knotted noose,
And watch my freedom atrophy,
Until I can barely move,
Another heart seduced by sorrow,
Afraid to leave its burning home,
Where hopeless thoughts become the laurels,
On which I rest my aching bones,
And now I'm sleeping in the fire,
Of the damned souls that came before,
Hell is a cage in heaven,
And we're the ones who shut the door.

We've been searching for arrival,
Inside this mash up of a place,
Where the destination is to notice,
That every demon is a saint,
For every burden on your shoulder,
Will pile higher than before,
Until your tired arms surrender,
And you carry them no more.

The Poet's Office

I've been offered the position of a Poet,
In the office high above the fields
where my ripe and naked heart
has labored carelessly,
And the daily quota of insecurity
was nowhere to be met.

I've worked hard for this promotion,
And even harder to decline it.

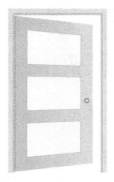

Tender waves caress the sand,
The ones you've ridden from the start,
A sun that gently warms your skin,
And also warms your heart,

A breeze that bears the weight of love,
Wherever it may go,
To angels flying high above,
And those swimming down below,

So dive into your crystal sea,
Beneath the shades of endless blue,
And you will find the perfect beach,
Is always here inside of you.

- The Beach

ALLEN JAMES

Empty Pages

Lucky is the man,
Whose pages lie unwritten,
Foolish are the ones,
Writing just to fill them,
Blackening the hollow,
Indeed it's *nothing* which they fear,
But once the paper's skin is broken,
The marks will never disappear,
Be close companions with your silence,
And you will have a friend of gold,
And every word will be born naturally,
From the womb inside your soul,
For each new sheet of solitude,
Is a temptress to withstand,
To let your tale be written,
By the heart before the hand,
And when the time will finally come,
To share the story you now write,
May you find a cherished moment,
In every letter of your life.

Paradise

Overhead the ocean realm,
Lies gently on the splendid sand,
And countless waves of coral shell,
Bring timeless grace back to the land,
Overhead eternal night,
The quiescent moon peers into sight,
And everything illuminates on hand.

Cloudless every day you fly
over the dusk of night,
Luring and insuring of my sight,
And from my dream I wake
to find I'm lost inside your eyes,
A thousand light blue trails
of paradise.

ACKNOWLEDGMENTS

To the woman who bears witness to every one of my trials and triumphs. I know my path wasn't easy, but you have blessed each and every step of my journey. Thank you, mom, for all the years of unconditional love and support. I couldn't have finished this book without it.

To *babulya* and *dedulya*, two beautiful souls who I'm proud to call my grandparents. Your wisdom continues to reach me not only in the form of words, but through the embodiment of who you are. Thank you for all your love and sincerity.

To my father, with whom I've recently had the chance to make amends with. I know it has been a long, continuous process for both of us, but I am so grateful for where we stand today. Thank you for all your support and all of the love you've shown me. I cherish it more than you can ever imagine.

To my dear friends, to whom I owe the world to. You have provided me with a warm home during so many cold nights. Thank you for bringing so much joy, compassion, and understanding into my life. It would take me another book just to express the gratitude you all deserve.

To the "strangers" who have reached out their hands in friendship over the years. Your kindness and affection continue to humble me. Thank you for being so generous with your hearts and teaching me the power of vulnerability.

And lastly, I'd like to thank you, the reader. I believe one of the most valuable things a person has to offer is their attention, and I am incredibly honored and grateful that you've chosen to give me yours.

Sincerely,
AJ

ABOUT THE AUTHOR

Allen James is a writer and musician from Brooklyn, NY. He was born in 1990 to Jewish-Ukrainian immigrants and grew up in Coney Island. *Hell Is A Cage In Heaven* is Allen's debut as an author and contains a collection of poems written throughout his life. Driven by its polarities, the book reveals a broad spectrum of topics and themes that narrate the nature of his story. The mind, in particular, is portrayed as both captor and liberator, as James shares his personal experiences with heaven, hell, and everything in between.

ByAllenJames.com

Instagram: @ByAllenJames

Facebook: Facebook.com/ByAllenJames

Twitter: @ByAllenJames

Made in United States
North Haven, CT
21 November 2021